Men should come with instruction booklets

A  Collection

by Cathy Guisewite

Andrews, McMeel & Parker
A Universal Press Syndicate Company
Kansas City • New York

5

6

18

21

22

25

26

27

28

29

30

35

37

40

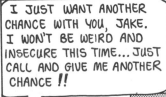

42

45

47

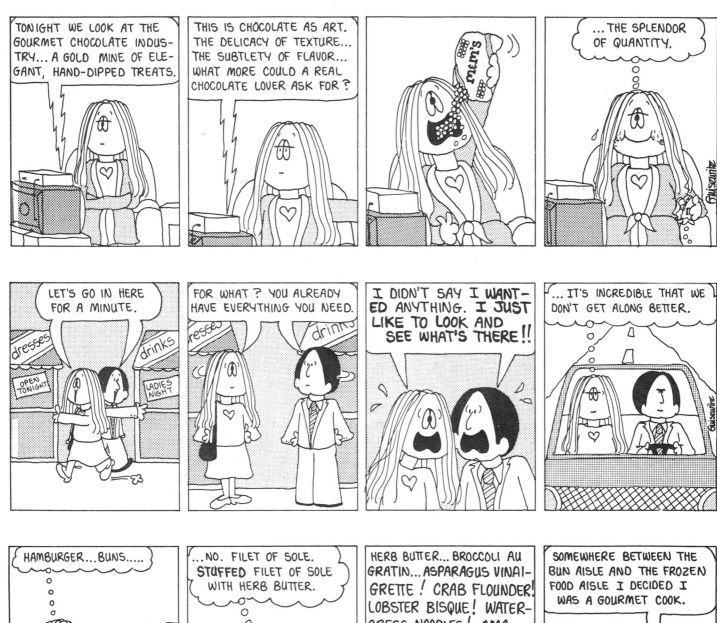

51

53

79

82

83

84

94

95

Panel 1:
AREN'T YOU A LITTLE EMBARRASSED TO GO BACK IN HERE?

WHY? THEY WON'T REMEMBER ME.

Panel 2:
CATHY, HOW IS IT THAT YOU EXPECT A CUTE MAN YOU GLANCED AT ONCE IN A RESTAURANT TO REMEMBER YOU SIX MONTHS LATER....

Panel 3:
...BUT YOU THINK A SALESPERSON YOU'VE BADGERED EVERY DAY FOR A WEEK IN A MICROWAVE STORE WON'T RECOGNIZE YOU??

Panel 4:
CAN I HELP IT IF I HAVE A SELECTIVE EGO?

Panel 5:
I'VE ALWAYS ADVISED YOU ON NUTRITION... YOU JOINED A "HEALTH CLUB," WHICH I KNOW NOTHING ABOUT.

Panel 6:
I'VE ALWAYS ADVISED YOU ON HOUSEKEEPING... YOU GOT A CAREER, WHICH I KNOW NOTHING ABOUT.

Panel 7:
I'VE ALWAYS ADVISED YOU ON COOKING... NOW YOU'RE BUYING A MICROWAVE, WHICH I KNOW NOTHING ABOUT!!

Panel 8:
...YOU'RE MAKING IT A REAL CHALLENGE TO BUTT IN ON YOUR LIFE.

Panel 9:
THERE'S A GREAT ORGANIZATION OF WOMEN IN MY OFFICE BUILDING I'D LIKE YOU TO MEET, CATHY!

FINE, ANDREA.

Panel 10:
...SOME NICE YOUNG COUPLES MOVED DOWN THE STREET FROM US, SWEETIE. I'D LOVE FOR YOU TO MEET THEM!

SURE, MOM.

Panel 11:
...A BUNCH OF US GET TOGETHER FOR AEROBICS AFTER WORK. YOU SHOULD COME AND MEET EVERYONE!

OKAY, JANET.

Panel 12:
MY YOUTH IS OVER, CHARLENE. I'M STARTING TO GET BLIND DATES WITH GROUPS.

101

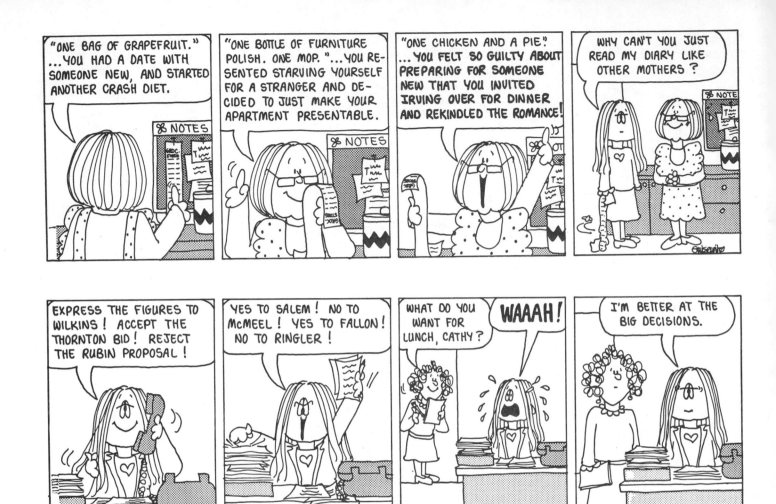

119

120

124